Memory Helper

for the book of

Colossians

King James Version

by Cindy Kolbo

WESTBOW
PRESS
A DIVISION OF THOMAS NELSON
& ZONDERVAN

Scripture taken from the King James Version of the Bible.

WestBow Press books may be ordered through booksellers or by contacting:

WestBow Press
A Division of Thomas Nelson & Zondervan
1663 Liberty Drive
Bloomington, IN 47403
www.westbowpress.com
1 (866) 928-1240

ISBN: 978-1-4908-4363-6 (sc)
ISBN: 978-1-4908-4364-3 (e)

Library of Congress Control Number: 2014913249

Printed in the United States of America.

WestBow Press rev. date: 09/22/2014

Deuteronomy 6:6, 7 "And these words, which I command thee this day, shall be in thine heart: And thou shalt teach them diligently unto thy children, and shalt talk of them when thou sittest in thine house, and when thou walkest by the way, and when thou liest down, and when thou risest up."

Nehemiah 8:8 "So they read in the book in the law of God distinctly, and gave the sense, and caused them to understand the reading."

These simple pages are presented as a tool to help you memorize Scripture. The goal of the picture is to give the reader something to hang the words on, while trying not to jeopardize the meaning of the verse. All Scripture is taken from the King James Version of the Bible.

The Strong's # refers to the number given for finding the definition of the original Greek word in *Strong's Exhaustive Concordance of the Bible* by James Strong.

Some Basics

 = crown = θ = God, especially God the Father in heaven

= Jesus = shown as a cross because of His willing sacrificial death for our sins

= a believer's heart, full of love for Jesus

= fire = sin = judgment = hell = punishment

=Satan or a demon

COLOSSIANS

Table of Contents

Colossians

Chapter One

Paul, an apostle of Jesus Christ by the will of God, and Timotheus our brother, (2) to the saints and faithful brethren in Christ which are at Colosse; Grace be unto you, and peace, from God our Father and the Lord Jesus Christ.

(3) We give thanks to God and the Father of our Lord Jesus Christ, praying always for you, (4) Since we heard of your faith in Christ Jesus, and the love which ye have to all the saints,

(5) For the hope which is laid up for you in heaven, whereof ye heard before in the word of the truth of the gospel; (6) which is come unto you, as it is in all the world; and bringeth forth fruit, as it doth also in you, since the day ye heard of it, and knew the grace of God in truth: (7) As ye also learned of Epaphras our dear fellow servant, who is for you a faithful minister of Christ; (8) Who also declared unto us your love in the Spirit.

(9) For this cause we also, since the day we heard it, do not cease to pray for you, and to desire that ye might be filled with the knowledge of his will in all wisdom and spiritual understanding;

(10) That ye might walk worthy of the Lord unto all pleasing, being fruitful in every good work, and increasing in the knowledge of God;

(11) Strengthened with all might, according to his glorious power, unto all patience and long-suffering with joyfulness;

(12) Giving thanks unto the Father, which hath made us meet to be partakers of the inheritance of the saints in light:

(13) Who hath delivered us from the power of darkness, and hath translated us into the kingdom of his dear Son:

(14) In whom we have redemption through his blood, even the forgiveness of sins:

(15) Who is the image of the invisible God, the firstborn of every creature:

(16) For by him were all things created, that are in heaven and that are in earth, visible and invisible, whether they be thrones, or dominions, or principalities, or powers: all things were created by him, and for him:

(17) And he is before all things, and by him all things consist:

(18) And he is the head of the body, the church: who is the beginning, the firstborn from the dead; that in all things he might have the preeminence.

(19) For it pleased the Father that in him should all fulness dwell; (20) And, having made peace through the blood of his cross, by him to reconcile all things unto himself; by him, I say, whether they be things in earth, or things in heaven.

(21) And you, that were sometime alienated and enemies in your mind by wicked works, yet now hath he reconciled
(22) In the body of his flesh through death, to present you holy and unblamable and unreprovable in his sight:
(23) If ye continue in the faith grounded and settled, and be not moved away from the hope of the gospel, which ye have heard, and which was preached to every creature which is under heaven; whereof I Paul am made a minister;

(24) Who now rejoice in my sufferings for you, and fill up that which is behind of the afflictions of Christ in my flesh for his body's sake, which is the church: (25) Whereof I am made a minister, according to the dispensation of God which is given to me for you, to fulfil the word of God;

(26) Even the mystery which hath been hid from ages and from generations, but now is made manifest to his saints:

(27) To whom God would make known what is the riches of the glory of this mystery among the Gentiles; which is Christ in you, the hope of glory: (28) Whom we preach, warning every man, and teaching every man in all wisdom; that we may present every man perfect in Christ Jesus: (29) Whereunto I also labor, striving according to his working, which worketh in me mightily.

In the picture:

This is a letter written by Paul to the believers in the church at Colosse, a city in Phrygia which is now a part of Turkey. Paul is an apostle of Jesus to the Gentiles (people who are not Jewish). He writes this letter from a prison, probably in Rome. Timothy is with Paul, but probably not a co-author. Paul wants to warn the Colossians against a heresy that combined Greek philosophy and Jewish legalism that said a person needs more than Jesus for salvation. Jesus (the cross) is sufficient!! The theme of the letter is that **Christ is all and in all** (the stamp). The date of the writing is on the post mark on the envelope.

The letter is addressed to the believers in Colosse (the saints are the faithful). Grace and peace are blessings from God made available to the believer because of the sacrifice of Jesus our Lord.

Word Definitions

1: 1-2 apostle = Strong's # 652 "a delegate; specifically an ambassador of the gospel; officially a commissioner of Christ (with miraculous powers)"

Timotheus = Strong's # 5095 "dear to God" (Timothy)

saints = Strong's # 40 "sacred (physically pure, morally blameless or religious, ceremonially consecrated)" believers; separated from sin and set apart to God

faithful = Strong's # 4103 "trustworthy"

brethren = Strong's # 80 "a brother (lit or fig) near or remote"   fellow believers

Colosse = Strong's # 2857 "a city in Phrygia"

grace = Strong's # 5485 "graciousness (as gratifying), of manner or act (abstract or concrete; lit or fig or spiritually; especially the divine influence upon the heart, and its reflection in the life; including gratitude)"

peace = Strong's # 1515 "peace (lit or fig), by implication, prosperity"

Lord = Strong's # 2962 "supreme in authority, controller; by implication, Mr. (as a respectful title)"

Paul, an apostle of Jesus Christ by the will of God, and Timotheus our brother, to the saints and faithful brethren In Christ which are at Colosse; Grace be unto you, and peace, from God our Father and the Lord Jesus Christ.

Colossians 1: 1-2

In the picture:

Paul and Timothy are praying. They are offering thanks to God for the Colossians. They are thankful that God has given the Colossians faith in Jesus. This is real faith because it is made of truth, obedience, and repentance. (Repentance is shown in the little bubble as a turning from the fire of sin to God.)

Their love for each other and other believers is shown as little hearts, full of love for Jesus, all connected to each other.

All this comes from God.

Word Definitions

1: 3-4   praying = Strong's # 4336 "to pray to God, supplicate, worship"

always = Strong's # 3842 "every when, at all times" (when Paul prayed for the Colossians, he always thanked God) Pray for people even when things are going well.

faith = Strong's # 4102 "persuasion, credence; moral conviction (of religious truth, or the truthfulness of God or a religious teacher), especially reliance upon Christ for salvation; abstract, constancy in such profession; by extension, the system of religious (Gospel) truth itself"
    True saving faith involves:
(1) truth... Your faith must be placed in someone worthy.
(2) obedience... Faith is related to obedience. Both words share the same root word.
(3) repentance... Repentance means a turning, that is a turning from sin, a turning to God, and a turning to serve Him.

love = Strong's # 26 "love, affection or benevolence; (plural) a love-feast" More than just emotional, the love that Christ gives is a sacrificial service to others in need. Love is commanded. (John 13:34-35)

We give thanks to God and the Father of our Lord Jesus Christ, praying always for you, Since we heard of your faith in Christ Jesus, and the love which ye have to all the saints,

Colossians 1: 3-4

In the picture:

The Bible is the Word of Truth, and from it we have the Gospel. This picture shows the 6 sides of the gospel mentioned in these verses:

1) The gospel is the believer's hope in heaven that is reserved for him
2) The gospel is for all the world, not just the Colossians
3) The gospel brings growth (just as a plant grows and bears fruit)
4) The gospel reveals the Grace of God (The sacrificial death of Christ gives forgiveness and eternal life.)
5) The gospel is learned and shared with others
6) The gospel yields love in the Spirit

Word Definitions

1: 5-8 hope = Strong's # 1680 "anticipate (with pleasure), expectation, confidence"

laid up = Strong's # 606 "reserved"

gospel = Strong's # 2098 "a good message, the gospel"

world = Strong's # 2889 "orderly arrangement, decoration; by implication, the world (in a wide or narrow sense, including its inhabitants; lit or fig)"

fruit = Strong's # 2592 "to be fertile"   fertile = able to produce much; rich in things that aid growth and development

knew = Strong's # 1921 "to know upon some mark, recognize; by implication, to become fully acquainted with, to acknowledge"

fellow servant = Strong's # 4889 "a co-slave, servitor or ministrant of the same master (human or divine)"

minister = Strong's # 1249 "an attendant, (generally) a waiter (at table or in other menial duties), specifically a Christian teacher and pastor, (technically a deacon or deaconess)"

declared = Strong's # 1213 "to make plain (by words)"

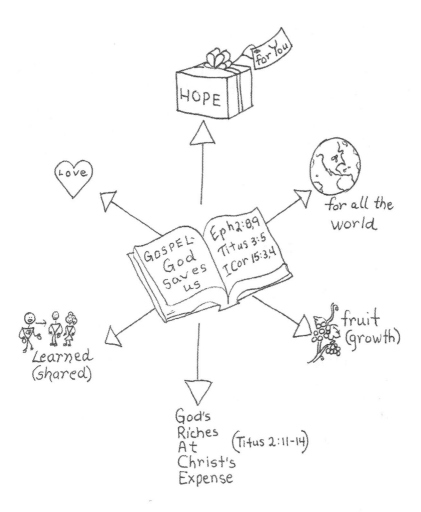

For the hope which is laid up for you in heaven, whereof ye
heard before in the word of the truth of the gospel; which is
come unto you, as it is in all the world; and bringeth forth
fruit, as it doth also in you, since the day ye heard of it, and
knew the grace of God in truth: As ye also learned of
Epaphras our dear fellow servant, who is for you a faithful
minister of Christ; Who also declared unto us your love in the
Spirit.

Colossians 1: 5-8

In the picture:

The two figures praying are Paul and Timothy. Paul has heard a good report about the Colossians, and he and Timothy continue to pray for them. All believers need the true knowledge from God. They are asking that God would fill the believers with the knowledge of His will. Knowledge of His will comes to us from a believing, submissive study of Scripture (II Tim 3:16, 17) and the Holy Spirit (I Cor 2:10-12). The knowledge of His will overflows into all wisdom and spiritual understanding.

The clock has no hands because there is no time limit on prayer.

Word Definitions

1: 9   cease = Strong's # 3973 "(pause); to stop...restrain, quit, desist, come to an end"

pray = Strong's # 4336 "to pray to God, supplicate, worship"

filled = Strong's # 4137 "to make replete, to cram (a net), level up (a hollow), or (fig) to furnish (or imbue, diffuse, influence), satisfy, execute (an office), finish (a period or task), verify (or coincide with a prediction)"

knowledge = Strong's # 1922 "recognition, (by implication) full discernment, acknowledgment" precise and correct knowledge, the knowledge of things ethical and divine

will = Strong's #2307 "a determination, choice (specifically, purpose, decree; abstract, volition) or (passive) inclination" what one wishes or has determined shall be done; of the purpose of God, to bless mankind through Christ

wisdom = Strong's # 4678 "wisdom (higher or lower, worldly or spiritual)"

spiritual = Strong's # 4152 "non-carnal, (humanly) ethereal (as opposed to gross), or (demoniacally) a spirit (concretely), or (divinely) supernatural, regenerate, religious"

understanding = Strong's # 4907 "a mental putting together, intelligence, or (concretely) the intellect"

Pray = ask

For this cause we also, since the day we heard it, do not cease to pray for you, and to desire that ye might be filled with the knowledge of his will in all wisdom and spiritual understanding;

Colossians 1: 9

In the picture:

Paul and Timothy are still praying. They are asking God to help the believers to walk worthy. The figure is walking in the path that describes a worthy walk from the Bible. The worthy walk has:

Humility (Ephesians 4:1-3)   Love (Ephesians 5:2)
Purity (Romans 13:13)   Truth (3 John 3-4)
Faith (II Corinthians 5:7)   Light (Ephesians 5:8)
Good Works (Ephesians 2:10)   Wisdom (Ephesians 5:15)
Contentedness(I Corinthians 7:17)
Different from the World (Ephesians 4:17-32)

Walking worthy pleases God, as shown in the smile on the crown.

Paul is also asking God to help them be fruitful. Some of the fruits of good work are in the tree. They are Praise (Heb 13:15), Righteousness (Heb 12:11), Giving (Ro 15:26-28), and the Fruit of the Spirit (Gal 5:22-23: love, joy, peace, longsuffering, kindness, goodness, faithfulness, gentleness, and self-control).

This path leads to an increase (the arrow pointing up) in the knowledge of God.

Word Definitions

1: 10   walk = Strong's # 4043 "to tread all around, walk at large (especially as proof of ability); to live, deport oneself, follow (as a companion or votary)"
votary = devoted, promised, consecrated by a vow
worthy = Strong's # 516 "appropriately"
fruitful = Strong's # 2592 "to be fertile (lit or fig)"
work = Strong's # 2041 "(to work); toil (as an effort or occupation), by implication, an act"
increasing = Strong's # 837 "to grow ("wax"), enlarge (lit or fig, actively or passively)"
knowledge = Strong's # 1922 "recognition, full discernment, acknowledgment"

12

That ye might walk worthy of the Lord unto all pleasing, being fruitful in every good work, and increasing in the knowledge of God;

Colossians 1: 10

In the picture:

Paul and Timothy are still praying. They are asking God to give the believers the knowledge of His will which will help them to be wise and understanding, walk worthy, be fruitful,(--from verses 9, 10), and in verse 11, we see that it gives us strength and joyful patience.

The crown is God and the knowledge and power come from Him through His Word and the Holy Spirit.

The figure is showing great strength. His muscles are God's might and His glorious power. These help him joyfully handle patience and longsuffering.

Word Definitions

1: 11   strengthened = Strong's # 1412 "to enable" continuous action

might = strength in action

power = Strong's # 2904 "vigor ["great"]"   the limitless power of God

patience = Strong's # 5281 "cheerful (or hopeful), endurance, constancy"

longsuffering = Strong's # 3115 "longanimity, forbearance or fortitude"

joyfulness = Strong's # 5479 "cheerfulness, calm delight"

Strengthened with all might, according to his glorious power, unto all patience and long-suffering with joyfulness;

Colossians 1: 11

In the picture:

Paul and Timothy are still praying but now they are thanking God. God the Father, shown as the crown, provides the power to make us fit through the cross of Jesus. The unbeliever is blind and a slave to sin, "having no hope and without God in the world" (Eph 2:11-13). Through the cross, God makes us fit to be a part of the Son's kingdom and share in the inheritance.

The document shows the inheritance. It includes those items listed. The light is shown as two candles, labeled truth and purity. (Light is sometimes a synonym for God's kingdom.)

The castle stands for the kingdom.

Word Definitions

1: 12   thanks = Strong's # 2168 "to be grateful, (act) to express gratitude (toward); specifically to say grace at a meal"

Father = from Judge to Father

meet = Strong's # 2427 "to enable, qualify"

to make sufficient, to authorize, to make fit

partakers = Strong's # 3310 "a portion, province, share or (abstract) participation"

inheritance = Strong's # 2819 "a die (for drawing chances); by implication, a portion (as if so secured), by extension, an acquisition (especially a patrimony, fig)"

The inheritance in Scripture includes

1) eternal life   (Matt 19:29)
2) the earth   (Matt 5:5)
3) the promises of God (Heb 6:12)

This inheritance is "incorruptible and undefiled and that does not fade away, reserved in heaven for you." (I Peter 1:4)

light = Strong's # 5457 "(to shine, or make manifest, especially by rays; luminousness (in the widest application, natural or artificial, abstract or concretely, lit or fig)"

Light in Scripture includes Truth (Ps 119:130) and Purity (Eph 5:8-14).

16

Giving thanks unto the Father, which hath made us
meet to be partakers of the inheritance of the saints
in light:

Colossians 1: 12

In the picture:

Paul and Timothy are still praying and giving thanks to God. God (the crown) has rescued/delivered us *through* the cross from the power of darkness (Satan's domain of slavery and blindness). We are delivered into the kingdom of the Son of His love, shown as a castle labeled with a heart.

Satan or a demon

Word Definitions

1: 13   delivered = Strong's # 4506 "(through the idea of a current); rush or draw (for oneself); rescue"

power = Strong's # 1849 "(in the sense of ability); privilege, force, capacity, competency, freedom, or mastery (concretely magistrate, superhuman, potentate, taken of control), delegated influence"

darkness = Strong's # 4655 "shadiness, obscurity (lit or fig)" deception, wickedness, Luke 22:53; I John 2:9, 11

translated = Strong's # 3179 "transfer, carry away, depose or (fig) exchange, seduce" conveyed, removed

kingdom = Strong's # 932 "royalty (abstractly) rule, or (concretely) a realm (lit or fig)"

Who hath delivered us from the power of
darkness, and hath translated us into the
kingdom of his dear Son:

Colossians 1: 13

19

In the picture:

Paul and Timothy are still praying. They are thanking God for paying the full ransom for believers *through* Jesus' blood on the cross. This redemption frees us from our chains and blindness and pardons us with forgiveness for our sins. Believers are granted the inheritance and placed in Christ's kingdom.

The blood is more than just the literal blood, just as the cross is more that just a structure. They stand for the willing sacrifice of Christ's sinless life, that is, the whole of His atoning work for us.

Word Definitions

1: 14   redemption = Strong's # 629 "(the act) ransom in full, (fig) riddance, or (specifically) Christian salvation" to deliver by payment of a ransom as in freeing slaves from bondage, emancipation

blood = Strong's # 129 "blood, lit (of men or animals), fig (the juice of grapes) or specifically (the atoning blood of Christ); by implication, bloodshed, also kindred"

forgiveness = Strong's # 859 "freedom; (fig) pardon" our sins sent away

In whom we have redemption through his blood,
even the forgiveness of sins:

Colossians 1: 14

In the picture:

The mirror shows that when we "see" Jesus we are "seeing" God. The crown (God) is looking into the mirror, and the image in the mirror is the cross that stands for Jesus.

Below the mirror is an equation that reads:

the cross *equals* Jesus *equals* the first place ribbon given as an award for superiority in excellence.

Word Definitions

1: 15   image = Strong's # 1504 "likeness, (lit) statue, profile, or (fig) representation, resemblance"
Jesus Christ is the exact likeness of God. He is God in human form, the perfect and complete image of God.
invisible = that cannot be seen, imperceptible by the sight
firstborn = Strong's # 4416 "(from 4413 foremost in time, place, order, or importance)" can mean chronologically, but more often refers to rank, the Preeminent One; exalted in rank above creation
creature = Strong's # 2937 "formation (properly the act; by implication the thing, lit or fig)"

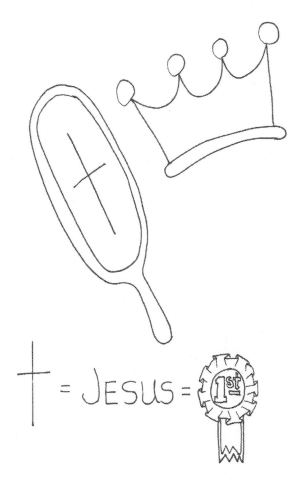

Who is the image of the invisible God,
the firstborn of every creature:

Colossians 1: 15

23

In the picture:

The picture shows a cross, Jesus, at the center of ALL things. He is God. He is the Preeminent One over ALL creation. By Him were ALL things created. ALL things were created through Him and for Him.

Here is a small sampling of some of the groups of things that Jesus created: families, marriage, men, women, girls, sisters, boys, brothers, dogs, cats, spiders, fish, birds, trees, flowers, clouds, rain, mountains, planets, stars, the sun, angels, music, light, warmth, water, air, fruit, and the church.

ALL fullness dwells in Him. He is able to reconcile ALL things to Himself because He has made peace through the blood of His cross.

Word Definitions

1: 16   Him = Jesus

created = Strong's # 2936 "to fabricate, found (form originally)"

heaven = Strong's # 3772 "the sky; by extension heaven (as the abode of God); by implication, happiness, power, eternity; specifically, the Gospel (Christianity)"

earth = Strong's # 1093 "soil; by extension, a region, or the solid part or the whole of the terrene globe (including the occupants in each application)"

Ranks of angels:

thrones = Strong's # 2362 "a stately seat ("throne"); by implication, power or (concretely) a potentate"

dominions = Strong's # 2963 "mastery, (concretely and collectively) rulers"

principalities = Strong's # 746 "a commencement, or (concretely) chief (in various applications of order, time, place, or rank)"

powers = Strong's # 1849 "privilege, force, capacity, competency, freedom, or mastery (concretely, magistrate, superhuman, potentate, taken of control), delegated influence"

For by him were all things created, that are in heaven and that are in earth, visible and invisible, whether they be thrones, or dominions, or principalities, or powers: all things were created by him, and for him:

Colossians 1: 16

25

In the picture:

The time line shows Jesus (the cross) as coming before the earth, before the sun, moon, and stars, and before the angels. He is eternal.

The center picture shows a cross (Jesus) holding together the atom. Scientists don't know why the positively charged protons of the nucleus hold together when like charges are supposed to repel each other. An explosion would by expected, but they are held together by a very powerful force!

Word Definitions

1: 17   He, Him = Jesus

  consist = Strong's # 4921 "to set together (by implication) to introduce (favorably), or (fig) to exhibit; intransitive, to stand near, or (fig) to constitute"

     constitute = to set, to fix, to enact, to establish, to form or compose; to give formal existence to; to make a thing what it is

     to hold together

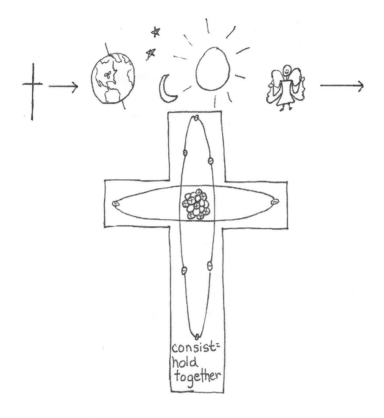

consist=
hold
together

And he is before all things,
and by him all things consist:

Colossians 1: 17

27

In the picture:

      As the church is topped by the cross (stands for Jesus) so also the body is topped by the head.

      Below that, the cross (Jesus) is the beginning. The two meanings are shown as:

            1) the firstborn of the dead, that is, the 1st of those with empty graves that will never see death again. This makes Jesus the source or originator of the church.

            2) Jesus as the leader, the highest in rank.

Word Definitions

1: 18   He = Jesus

head = Strong's # 2776 "the head (as the part most rapidly taken hold of)"
    controls every part of the body, gives it life and direction

body = Strong's # 4983 "the body (as a sound whole), used in a very wide application, lit or fig"

church = Strong's # 1577 "a calling out, (concretely) a popular meeting, especially a religious congregation (Jewish synagogue, or Christian community of members on earth or saints in heaven or both)"

beginning = two meanings: 1) source or originator
                                2) chief position or highest in rank

firstborn = Strong's # 4416 "first born" highest in rank

preeminence = Strong's # 4409 "to be first (in rank or influence)"

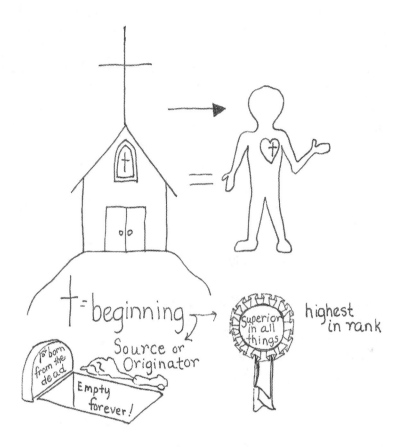

And he is the head of the body, the church: who is the
beginning, the firstborn from the dead; that in all
things he might have the preeminence.

Colossians 1: 18

In the picture:

The smile on the crown shows that God is pleased. The crown on the cross shows that all the fullness of God is also present in Jesus (the cross). Jesus breaks through the barrier of sin that separates us from God and changes us from an enemy to a friend at peace with God. (He reconciles us to God.) All creation, both things on earth and things in heaven, has been affected by sin. All things in the created universe will submit to Jesus either in the judgment against them or *in* peace *through* the blood of His cross in salvation.

Word Definitions

1: 19-20   pleased = Strong's # 2106 "to think well of, approve (an act), specifically, to approbate (a person or thing)"
Him = Jesus
fulness = Strong's # 4138 "repletion or completion, what fills (as contents, supplement, copiousness, multitude), or what is filled (as container, performance, period)"
all fulness = all of God's power and attributes
dwell = Strong's # 2730 "to house permanently, reside (lit or fig)"
peace = Strong's # 1517 "to be a peacemaker, to harmonize"
cross = Strong's # 4716 "a stake or post (as set upright), (specifically) a pole or cross (as an instrument of capital punishment), fig, exposure to death, self-denial; by implication, the atonement of Christ"
reconcile = Strong's # 604 "to reconcile fully"
to call back into union and friendship the affections which have been alienated

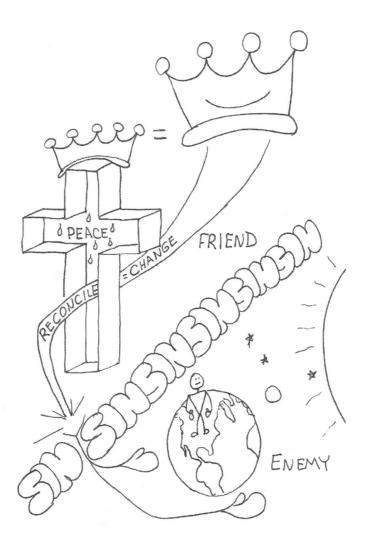

For it pleased the Father that in him should all fulness dwell; And, having made peace through the blood of his cross, by him to reconcile all things unto himself; by him, I say, whether they be things in earth, or things in heaven.

Colossians 1: 19-20

31

In the picture:

The unbeliever on the edge of a cliff is cut off from God because his mind is filled with wicked works, and his heart has no love for the Lord and no desire for God. Only through Jesus can he be made friends with God. God's penalty for sin must be paid before reconciliation takes place. Jesus Christ's death was that perfect offering (Jesus is shown with a "body" on the cross to show His death was real and physical). You cannot pay your own penalty, because you are guilty, helpless, and ungodly.

Through the cross of Jesus, you are presented holy, blameless, and above reproach (the banners waved by the saved figure) to God. Jesus holds the believer immoveable on top of the solid rocks in the path of faith and resting in the hope of the gospel. Paul, the minister in the bubble in the upper left, is preaching this message everywhere he goes (2 Cor 5:17-21).

Word Definitions

1: 21-23 alienated = Strong's # 526 "to estrange away, to be non-participant"

wicked = Strong's # 4190 "hurtful, evil (properly in effect or influence, fig., calamitous; also (passively) ill, diseased, by extension, culpable, derelict, vicious; mischief, malice, guilt, the devil, or sinners"

he, his = Jesus

flesh = Strong's # 4561 "flesh (as stripped of skin), (strictly) the meat of an animal (as food), or (by ext) the body (as opposed to the soul or spirit, or as the symbol of what is external or as the means of kindred) or (by imp) human nature (with its frailties [physical or moral] and passions) or (spec) a human being (as such)"

present = Strong's # 3936 "to stand beside, to exhibit, proffer, (spec) recommend, (fig) substantiate; or to be at hand (or ready), aid"

settled = Strong's # 1476 "sedentary, (by implication) immoveable" steadfast

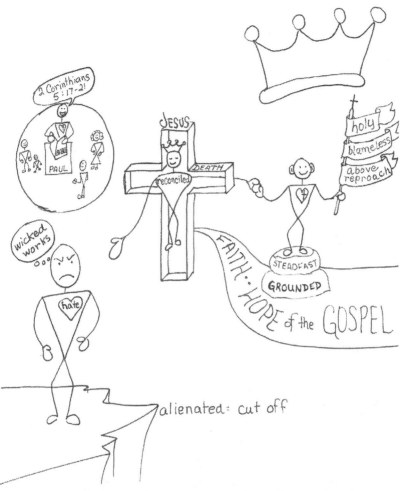

And you, that were sometime alienated and enemies in your mind by wicked works, yet now hath he reconciled In the body of his flesh through death, to present you holy and unblamable and unreprovable in his sight: If ye continue in the faith grounded and settled, and be not moved away from the hope of the gospel, which ye have heard, and which was preached to every creature which is under heaven; whereof I Paul am made a minister;   Colossians 1: 21-23

In the picture:

Even though he is a prisoner, Paul is joyful because he is obeying God and telling others about the Word of God (he is sending a letter to the Colossians). Unbelievers hate Paul because he loves Jesus. Paul is getting the hate that the world feels toward Jesus. This hate is never satisfied.

God, the crown, called Paul and gave him the desire and the job of teaching others His Word.

Word Definitions

1: 24-25   rejoice = Strong's # 5463 "to be cheerful, calmly happy or well off; impersonally, especially as a salutation (on meeting or parting) 'be well'"

sufferings = Strong's # 3804 "something undergone, hardship or pain; an emotion or influence"

fill up = Strong's # 466 "to supplement"

that which is behind = Strong's # 5303 "a deficit, specially poverty"

The lacking mentioned in the verse is not with Jesus, but with the amount of suffering and torment the world wanted to pour out on Jesus, but was unable to since He is gone. This hate is now focused on those who love Jesus.

afflictions = Strong's # 2347 "pressure (lit or fig)"

church = Strong's # 1577 "a calling out (concretely) a popular meeting, especially a religious congregation (Jewish synagogue, Christian community of members on earth or saints in heaven or both)"

dispensation = Strong's # 3622 "administration (of a household or estate); specifically, a (religious) 'economy'"

fulfill = Strong's # 4137 "to make replete (lit) to cram (a net), level up (a hollow), or (fig) to furnish (or imbue, diffuse, influence), satisfy, execute (an office), finish (a period or task), verify (or coincide with a prediction)"

Who now rejoice in my sufferings for you, and fill up that which is behind of the afflictions of Christ in my flesh for his body's sake, which is the church: Whereof I am made a minister, according to the dispensation of God which is given to me for you, to fulfill the word of God;

Colossians 1: 24-25

35

In the picture:

Paul is revealing the mystery (the question mark) that stands behind the "secret curtain." This mystery was hidden from generations--from Adam and Eve (the two figures in skins beside the apple) and from the Old Testament followers (the bearded fellow). They didn't know the mystery that God has now revealed to His saints.

Word Definitions

1: 26   mystery = Strong's # 3466 "a secret or 'mystery' (through the idea of silence imposed by initiation into religious rites)"   a truth, hidden until now

hid = Strong's # 613 "to conceal away, (fully); fig, to keep a secret"

ages = Strong's # 165 "an age; by extension, perpetuity, (also past); by implication, the world; specifically, (Jewish) or Messianic period (present or future)"

generations = Strong's # 1074 "a generation; by implication, an age (the period or the persons)"

manifest = Strong's # 5319 "to render apparent (lit or fig)"

Even the mystery which hath been hid from ages and from generations, but now is made manifest to his saints:

Colossians 1: 26

In the picture:

The mystery is revealed! The curtain opens to show the saints a treasure chest (the riches) containing the heart with CHRIST IN YOU, THE HOPE OF GLORY written inside, even to the Gentiles! Paul is preaching about Jesus. He is warning and teaching every man (the figures) *in* all wisdom. God gives power to His people so that believers will use their ears to hear the message to love and obey Jesus fully and completely (A+).

Paul works hard because God works mightily through us.

Word Definitions

1: 27-29   riches = Strong's # 4149 "wealth (as fulness) lit. money, possessions, or (fig.) abundance, riches, (spec.) valuable bestowment"

Gentiles = Strong's # 1484 "a race (as of the same habit), a tribe; specifically a foreign (non-Jewish) one (usually by implication pagan)"

hope = Strong's # 1680 "(to anticipate, usually with pleasure); expectation or confidence"

preach = Strong's # 2605 "to proclaim, promulgate"

warning = Strong's # 3560 "to put in mind, to caution or reprove gently"

perfect = Strong's # 5046 "complete (in various applications of labor, growth, mental and moral character), completeness"

labor = Strong's # 2872 "to feel fatigue; by implication to work hard"

striving = Strong's # 75 "to struggle, lit. (to compete for a prize), fig. (to contend with an adversary), or generally (to endeavor to accomplish something)"

working = Strong's # 1753 "efficiency (energy)"

mightily =Strong's # 1411 "force (lit or fig); specifically miraculous power (usually by implication a miracle itself)"

To whom God would make known what is the riches of the glory of this mystery among the Gentiles; which is Christ in you, the hope of glory: Whom we preach, warning every man, and teaching every man in all wisdom; that we may present every man perfect in Christ Jesus: Whereunto I also labor, striving according to his working, which worketh in me mightily.

Colossians 1: 27-29

Colossians

Chapter Two

For I would that ye knew what great conflict I have for you, and for them at Laodicea, and for as many as have not seen my face in the flesh;

(2) That their hearts might be comforted, being knit together in love, and unto all riches of the full assurance of understanding, to the acknowledgment of the mystery of God, and the Father, and of Christ; (3) In whom are hid all the treasures of wisdom and knowledge.

(4) And this I say, lest any man should beguile you with enticing words. (5) For though I be absent in the flesh, yet am I with you in the spirit, joying and beholding your order, and the steadfastness of your faith in Christ.

(6) As ye have therefore received Christ Jesus the Lord, so walk ye in him: (7) Rooted and built up in him, and stablished in the faith, as ye have been taught, abounding therein with thanksgiving.

(8) Beware lest any man spoil you through philosophy and vain deceit, after the tradition of men, after the rudiments of the world, and not after Christ. (9) For in him dwelleth all the fulness of the Godhead bodily. (10) And ye are complete in him, which is the head of all principality and power:

(11) In whom also ye are circumcised with the circumcision made without hands, in putting off the body of the sins of the flesh by the circumcision of Christ; (12) Buried with him in baptism, wherein also ye are risen with him through the faith of the operation of God, who hath raised him from the dead.

(13) And you, being dead in your sins and the uncircumcision of your flesh, hath he quickened together with him, having forgiven you all trespasses; (14) Blotting out the handwriting of ordinances that was against us, which was contrary to us, and took it out of the way, nailing it to his cross; (15) And having spoiled principalities and powers, he made a show of them openly, triumphing over them in it.

(16) Let no man therefore judge you in meat, or in drink, or in respect of a holyday, or of the new moon, or of the sabbath days: (17) Which are a shadow of things to come; but the body is of Christ.

(18) Let no man beguile you of your reward in a voluntary humility and worshiping of angels, intruding into those things which he hath not seen, vainly puffed up by his fleshly mind, (19) And not holding the Head, from which all the body by joints and bands having nourishment ministered, and knit together, increaseth with the increase of God.

(20) Wherefore if ye be dead with Christ from the rudiments of the world, why, as though living in the world, are ye subject to ordinances, (21) (Touch not; taste not; handle not; (22) Which all are to perish with the using;) after the commandments and doctrines of men? (23) Which things have indeed a show of wisdom in will-worship, and humility, and neglecting of the body; not in any honor to the satisfying of the flesh.

In the picture:

Paul is concerned for the Colossians and the neighboring Laodiceans and even those believers he has never met (US!). Paul is exerting great effort in his praying (He is sweating).

Word Definitions

2: 1   great = Strong's # 2245 "as big as, (interjection) how much"

conflict = Strong's # 73 "a place of assembly (as if led), (by implication) a contest (held there); fig, an effort or anxiety"   agony

Laodicea = Strong's # 2993 "Chief city of Phrygia, a place in Asia Minor"

face = Strong's # 4383 "the front, (as being toward view), the countenance, aspect, appearance, surface; by implication, presence, person"

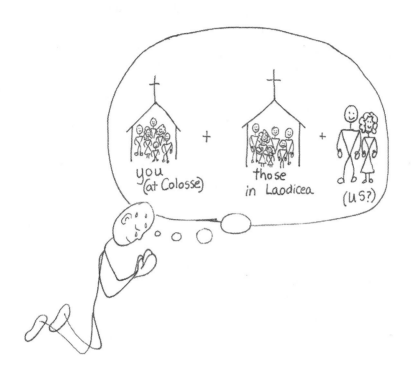

For I would that ye knew what great
conflict I have for you, and for them at
Laodicea, and for as many as have not seen my
face in the flesh;

Colossians 2: 1

In the picture:

    There are three pictures here:

      1) the man's head = a strong heart. The heart is not just the emotions (which are usually called "bowels" in the Bible). The heart is a picture of the thinking part of a man, the inner man, the center of life.

      2) the chain of strong hearts full of love (knitted)

      3) the man scaling the mountain of riches atop the Bible.

    Jesus is the mystery of God Himself revealed. He is God in human form, in which are hidden all the treasures of wisdom and knowledge. Here is a picture of all the treasure chests of riches that can be gained through Christ, that is, wisdom and knowledge, and all the riches of the assurance of understanding.

Word Definitions

2: 2-3 hearts = Strong's # 2588 "the heart, (fig) the thoughts or feelings (mind); also (by analogy) the middle"

comforted = Strong's # 3870 "to call near, invite, invoke (by imploration, hortation or consolation)" strengthened

knit = Strong's # 4822 "to drive together, unite (in association or affection), (mentally) to infer, show, teach"

riches = Strong's # 4149 "wealth (as fulness) (lit) money, possessions, or (fig) richness, (specifically) valuable bestowment"

full assurance = Strong's # 4136 "entire confidence"

understanding = Strong's # 4907 "a mental putting together, intelligence or (concretely) the intellect"

applying Biblical principles to everyday life

acknowledgment = Strong's # 1922 "recognition, (by implication) full discernment"

hid = Strong's # 614 "secret; by implication, treasured"

That their hearts might be comforted, being knit together in love, and unto all riches of the full assurance of understanding, to the acknowledgment of the mystery of God, and the Father, and of Christ; In whom are hid all the treasures of wisdom and knowledge.

Colossians 2: 2-3

In the picture:

      Paul is in prison (the prison bars are behind him). He is writing "Truth" to the church. He is warning them not to be fooled by the persuasive words of the false teachers. Even though he is in prison, Paul's thoughts (the bubble) show that he is still thinking of them. He smiles because he sees their good order; they are holding their positions. He uses military terms to show that they are standing firm against the enemy.

Word Definitions

2: 4-5   beguile = Strong's # 3884 "to misreckon, delude"
          delude = to mislead the mind or judgment
   enticing = Strong's # 4086 "persuasive language"
          influencing the mind or passions
   joying = Strong's # 5463 "to be 'cheer'ful, calmly happy or
          well-off; impersonal, especially as salutation (on meeting
          or parting), be well"
   order = Strong's # 5010 "regular arrangement, (in time) fixed
          succession (of rank or character), official dignity"
   steadfastness = Strong's # 4733 "something established,
          (abstract) confirmation (stability)"

     [Both "order" and "steadfastness" are military terms depicting a solid rank of soldiers drawn up for battle.]

And this I say, lest any man should beguile
you with enticing words. For though I be absent in
the flesh, yet am I with you in the spirit, joying
and beholding your order, and the steadfastness of
your faith in Christ.

Colossians 2: 4-5

In the picture:

The figure shown has a heart filled with love for Jesus (the cross in his heart). He is walking *in* Jesus (the cross). Because he has roots going deep into the cross, this builds him up (the extra layer around his body). He is stable in his faith because Paul has taught him Truth. His response is to overflow with "thank you" and praise to the Lord.

Word Definitions

2: 6-7   therefore = "because of what has just been said"

received = Strong's # 3880 "to receive near, associate oneself (in any familiar or intimate act or relation); by analogy, to assume an office; fig, to learn"

walk = Strong's # 4043 "to tread all around, walk at large (especially as proof of ability) fig, to live, deport oneself, follow (as a companion or votary)"

votary = One devoted, consecrated, or engaged by a vow or promise, hence more generally, one devoted, given, or addicted to some particular service, worship, study, or state of life.

rooted = Strong's # 4492 "to root (fig, become stable)"

built up = Strong's # 2026 "to build upon (fig) to rear up"

stablished = Strong's # 950 "to stabilitate (fig)" to make stable

abounding = Strong's # 4052 "to super abound (in quantity or quality), be in excess, be superfluous; also to cause to super abound or excel"

thanksgiving = Strong's # 2169 "gratitude; grateful language (to God, as an act of worship)"

As ye have therefore received
Christ Jesus the Lord, so walk ye in him:
Rooted and built up in him, and stablished
in the faith, as ye have been taught,
abounding therein with thanksgiving.

Colossians 2: 6-7

In the picture:

Paul is warning the figure not to fall for the lies of the false teachers because Satan is behind these lies. He wants to carry you off, as if kidnapped or robbed (see the club and bag). Some tricks of Satan are:

1) "Philosophy" is shown as a big head. Don't fall for the illusion of "intellect" apart from Christ.

2) The "tradition of men" is the lure of the sign stating that Generations have always thought this way. Just because the idea has been around for a long time doesn't make it true!

3) The "rudiments" are the ABC's of life. The principles that are too simplistic and silly, and don't really stand up to scrutiny because they are of the world and not according to Christ. Only He is the source of mature, spiritual truth.

We must walk in Christ, to follow Him because:

1) He is forever and fully God (shown as a crown on the cross). He is God in the flesh.

2) Only Christ can make you complete, to fill the empty hole in you and furnish you with His Truth and His nature (2 Peter 1:4).

3) He is the Head of the angels ("principality and power" referring to the realm of angels). They obey Him and bow before Him. We should do the same.

Word Definitions

2: 8-10   spoil = Strong's # 4812 "to lead away as booty, (fig, seduce)"   rob or kidnap

philosophy = Strong's # 5385 "philosophy, (specifically) Jewish sophistry"   sophistry = fallacious reasoning, reasoning sound in appearance only; "higher" knowledge, mystical

tradition = Strong's # 3862 "transmission, a precept; specifically the Jewish traditionary law"   given from one generation to another (perpetual error)

rudiments = Strong's # 4747 "something orderly in arrangement, a serial (basal, fundamental, initial) constituent (lit)," childish, things in a row, the letters of the alphabet, as in the ABC's; basic principles

50

Beware lest any man spoil you through philosophy and vain deceit, after the tradition of men, after the rudiments of the world, and not after Christ. For in him dwelleth all the fulness of the Godhead bodily. And ye are complete in him, which is the head of all principality and power:

Colossians 2: 8-10

In the picture:

    Two pictures here:

  1) "In Whom" means "In Christ." This is shown as being inside the cross that symbolizes Jesus Christ. Circumcision is shown as a cutting away of the sin in our heart. It is not the rite, but the cleansing of Christ that we need.

  2) "Buried with Him" and "raised with Him" are shown as the man being hugged by the cross and by the power of God in the symbolism of baptism, first put under then raised up in union with Christ. It is not the rite of water baptism, but the power of God that raises us from death.

Word Definitions

2: 11-12 circumcised = Strong's # 4059 "to cut around, to
      circumcise"

    buried = Strong's # 4916 "to inter in company with (fig) to
      assimilate spiritually (to Christ by a sepulture as to sin)"
      sepulture = the act of depositing the dead body of a
      human being in the grave

    risen = Strong's # 4891 "to rouse (from death) in company
      with, (fig) to revivify (spiritually) in resemblance to"

    raised =Strong's # 1453 "to waken, rouse (lit from sleep,
      from sitting or lying, from disease, from death; or fig,
      from obscurity, inactivity, ruin, non-existence)"

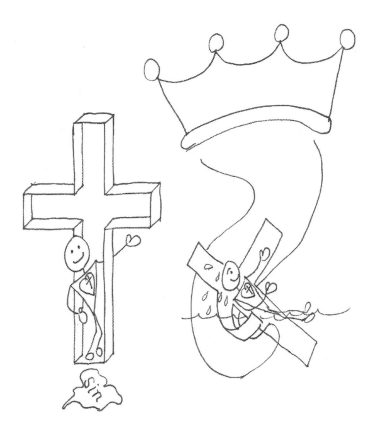

In whom also ye are circumcised with the circumcision made without hands, in putting off the body of the sins of the flesh by the circumcision of Christ; Buried with him in baptism, wherein also ye are risen with him through the faith of the operation of God, who hath raised him from the dead.

Colossians 2: 11-12

In the picture:

The grave with the tombstone labeled "Me" pictures you in your unbelieving state with all your sins, trespasses, and your heart still unclean with all its love of sin. You are truly dead in your response to God. But Jesus (the cross) has taken you out of that grave and forgiven you! He has taken the list of the sins against you and nailed it to His cross where His blood has wiped out the record of your sin.

With the penalty for your sin paid, Satan and his demons (the ugly figures) are disarmed. Before God and all, they are the losers. Their charge against you is now empty. You are clean, and your heart is filled with love for Jesus (the cross in your heart). Jesus has accomplished the victory for you when you were powerless to do it for yourself.

Word Definitions

2: 13-15   sins = Strong's # 3900 "a side-slip (lapse or deviation); unintentional error or willful transgression"
transgression = breaking a law, command

uncircumcision = Strong's # 203 "the prepuce; by implication, an uncircumcised (Gentile, fig, unregenerate) state or person"

quickened = Strong's # 4806 "to reanimate conjointly with (fig)"   made alive

forgiven = Strong's # 5483 "to grant us a favor, gratuitously, in kindness, pardon, or rescue"

principalities and powers = the ranks of fallen angels (Satan and his demons are the losers.)   Romans 8:37-39

openly = Strong's # 1722 "denoting (fixed) position (in place, time, or state)" + Strong's # 3954 "all outspokenness, frankness, bluntness, publicity; by implication, assurance" public spectacle

triumphing = Strong's # 2358 "to make an acclamatory procession, (fig) to conquer or (by Hebrew) to give victory"   complete victory

54

And you, being dead in your sins and the
uncircumcision of your flesh, hath he
quickened together with him, having forgiven
you all trespasses; Blotting out the
handwriting of ordinances that was against
us, which was contrary to us, and took it out
of the way, nailing it to his cross; And
having spoiled principalities and powers, he
made a show of them openly, triumphing over
them in it.

Colossians 2: 13-15

In the picture:

Here is a believer being judged by another person to see if he is following all of the extra rules. There is a long list of rules! For some "churches" it is questionable if Christ is really their Head. They enforce "Church Rules" that are to their liking, but are just a shadow of real love for Jesus.

Word Definitions

2: 16-17   judge = Strong's # 2919 "to distinguish, decide (mentally or judicially); by implication, to try, condemn, punish" Legalism is useless and dangerous because it attempts to control the outward behavior without cleansing the heart.

meat = Strong's # 1035 "eating (lit or fig), by extension, food (lit or fig)"

holyday = Strong's # 1859 "a festival"

sabbath = Strong's # 4521 "the Sabbath or day of weekly repose from secular avocations (also the observance or institution itself); by extension a se'nnight, the interval between 2 Sabbaths; likewise the plural in all the above applications" The sign to Israel of the Old Covenant.

shadow = Strong's # 4639 "shade or shadow (lit or fig (darkness of error or an adumbration))"

The shadow isn't the real substance. These things just pointed to Jesus. Christianity is not just rules, but loving and obeying Jesus.

Let no man therefore judge you in meat, or in drink, or in respect of a holyday, or of the new moon, or of the sabbath days: Which are a shadow of things to come; but the body is of Christ.

Colossians 2: 16-17

In the picture:

Paul is warning against questionable religion (note the question mark on top of the church).

1) False humility is really ugly, spiritual pride.

2) The worship of angels, a heresy of the region, robs God of His rightful place in our hearts.

3) The books stand for the many visions supposedly from God. These lead to wrong beliefs and wrong worship as they try to improve upon the Bible. Mysticism is the lure that there is a deeper spirituality to be found inside ourselves rather than reasoning from Scripture. Many consider their "visions" an easier, more direct path to God, but there is no substance.

4) The grandeur of ceremony can make us feel important and side-track us from truth.

In reality, they have lost their hold on Christ, the Head. God's power strengthens us only through Christ. The hearts under the true church are rooted in Scripture and knit together for growth from God. God grows you when you hold fast to Jesus.

Word Definitions

2: 18-19   beguile = Strong's # 2603   "to award the prize against, (fig) to defraud (of salvation)"   defraud = take money, rights, etc., away by fraud, cheat

voluntary = Strong's # 2309 "to determine (as an actual option from subjective impulse), choose or prefer (lit or fig); by (implication) to wish, be inclined to (sometimes adv gladly); impersonally for the future tense, to be about to; by Hebrew, to delight in"   false humility

vainly = Strong's # 1500 "idly, without reason (or effect)"

puffed up = Strong's # 5448 "to inflate, (fig) make proud (haughty)"

joints = Strong's # 860 "a ligament (as fastening)"

increase = Strong's # 838 "growth"

Let no man beguile you of your reward in a
voluntary humility and worshiping of angels,
intruding into those things which he hath not seen,
vainly puffed up by his fleshly mind, And not
holding the Head, from which all the body by joints
and bands having nourishment ministered, and knit
together, increaseth with the increase of God.

Colossians 2: 18-19

In the picture:

The believer has been raised with Jesus above the things of this world. Why imprison yourself in man-made religion that will be of no worth to you?

Word Definitions

2: 20-23   subject = Strong's # 1379 "to prescribe by statute, to submit to ceremonial rule"

touch = Strong's # 680 "to attach oneself to"

taste = Strong's # 1089 "to taste; by implication, to eat; fig, to experience (good or ill)"

handle = Strong's # 2345 "to manipulate, have to do with; by implication, to injure"

perish = Strong's # 5356 "decay, ruin (spontaneous or inflicted)"

commandments = Strong's # 1778 "an injunction, religious precept"

doctrines = Strong's # 1319 "instruction (the function or the information)"

will-worship = Strong's # 1479 "voluntary (arbitrary and unwarranted) piety, sanctimony"   self-imposed religion

neglecting = Strong's # 857 "unsparingness, austerity (asceticism)"   asceticism = extreme self-denial for spiritual gain; to free the spirit from the evil body; a useless, godless practice

honor = Strong's # 5092 "value, money paid, or (concrete and collect) valuables; by analogy, esteem (especially of the highest degree), or the dignity itself"

satisfying = Strong's # 4140 "a filling up, (fig) gratification" indulgence

Wherefore if ye be dead with Christ from the rudiments of the world, why, as though living in the world, are ye subject to ordinances, (Touch not; taste not; handle not; Which all are to perish with the using;) after the commandments and doctrines of men? Which things have indeed a show of wisdom in will-worship, and humility, and neglecting of the body; not in any honor to the satisfying of the flesh.

Colossians 2: 20-23

Colossians
Chapter Three

If ye then be risen with Christ, seek those things which are above, where Christ sitteth on the right hand of God. (2) Set your affection on things above, not on things on the earth. (3) For ye are dead, and your life is hid with Christ in God. (4) When Christ, who is our life, shall appear, then shall ye also appear with him in glory.

(5) Mortify therefore your members which are upon the earth; fornication, uncleanness, inordinate affection, evil concupiscence, and covetousness, which is idolatry: (6) For which things' sake the wrath of God cometh on the children of disobedience: (7) In the which ye also walked sometime, when ye lived in them.

(8) But now ye also put off all these; anger, wrath, malice, blasphemy, filthy communication out of your mouth. (9) Lie not one to another, seeing that ye have put off the old man with his deeds; (10) And have put on the new man, which is renewed in knowledge after the image of him that created him:

(11) Where there is neither Greek nor Jew, circumcision nor uncircumcision, Barbarian, Scythian, bond nor free: but Christ is all, and in all.

(12) Put on therefore, as the elect of God, holy and beloved, bowels of mercies, kindness, humbleness of mind, meekness, long-suffering; (13) Forbearing one another, and forgiving one another, if any man have a quarrel against any: even as Christ forgave you, so also do ye. (14) And above all these things put on charity, which is the bond of perfectness.

(15) And let the peace of God rule in your hearts, to the which also ye are called in one body; and be ye thankful.

(16) Let the word of Christ dwell in you richly in all wisdom; teaching and admonishing one another in psalms and hymns and spiritual songs, singing with grace in your hearts to the Lord.

(17) And whatsoever ye do in word or deed, do all in the name of the Lord Jesus, giving thanks to God and the Father by him.

(18) Wives, submit yourselves unto your own husbands, as it is fit in the Lord.

(19) Husbands, love your wives, and be not bitter against them.

(20) Children, obey your parents in all things: for this is well-pleasing unto the Lord.

(21) Fathers, provoke not your children to anger, lest they be discouraged.

(22) Servants, obey in all things your masters according to the flesh; not with eyeservice, as menpleasers; but in singleness of heart, fearing God:

(23) And whatsoever ye do, do it heartily, as to the Lord, and not unto men; (24) Knowing that of the Lord ye shall receive the reward of the inheritance: for ye serve the Lord Christ. (25) But he that doeth wrong shall receive for the wrong which he hath done: and there is no respect of persons.

In the picture:

The believer (his heart is full of love for Christ) is "floating" above the ground because he has been raised with Christ. He is seeking the things which are above (which are the things of heaven). The Bible is the only way to know what those things are. Christ is the one sitting on the throne at the right hand of God the Father (shown as a crown). The believer is hidden in Christ (the cross), even though his grave is on the earth. The lines radiating out from Christ and the hidden man and God stand for (very apparent) glory.

Word Definitions

3: 1-4   risen = Strong's # 4891 "to rouse (from death) in company with"   At the moment of your conversion, you became alive with Jesus to understand spiritual truths. Better translated, "Since you were raised..."

seek = Strong's # 2212 "to worship"

right hand of God = a place of honor and majesty

affection = Strong's # 5426 "to exercise the mind, entertain or have a sentiment or opinion, to be (mentally) disposed (more or less earnestly in a certain direction)"

set your mind = think! Heavenly thoughts can only come by understanding heavenly realities from Scripture.

dead = in the past; It was Jesus Christ's death that paid the penalty for your sin so you will arise with Him to new life. John MacArthur explains that this rich phrase has a three fold meaning:

    1) a shared spiritual life with Jesus and God
        (I Cor 2:17; II Pet 1:4)
    2) the world can't understand it (I Cor 2:14)
    3) believers are eternally secure with access to God's blessings and protected from all spiritual enemies
        (John 10:28; Rom. 8:31-39; Heb. 7:25; I Peter 1:4)

appear = Strong's # 5319 "to render apparent" second coming of Jesus (Rev. 19:11-13, 15-16)

If ye then be risen with Christ, seek those things which are above, where Christ sitteth on the right hand of God. Set your affection on things above, not on things on the earth. For ye are dead, and your life is hid with Christ in God. When Christ, who is our life, shall appear, then shall ye also appear with him in glory.

Colossians 3: 1-4

In the picture:

  The man is cutting off (killing) parts of his body (like warts). These warts are named. He once lived with his warts and loved them, but now his heart loves Jesus.

  The wrath of God is shown as lightening bolts from the crown. The sons of disobedience have just let their warts grow even though God's judgment is upon them. Their hearts are only filled with themselves, "Me".

Word Definitions

3: 5-7 mortify = Strong's # 3499 "to deaden, to subdue"
   kill

 members = Strong's # 3196 "a limb or part of the body"

 fornication = Strong's # 4202 "harlotry (including adultery
   and incest); fig, idolatry" harlotry = prostitution

 uncleanness = Strong's # 167 "impurity (the quality)"

 inordinate affection = Strong's # 3806 "suffering, a passion
   (especially concupiscence)" concupiscence = eagerly
   desirous, lustful, sensual

 evil desire = Strong's # 2556 "worthless (intrinsically),
   depraved, or injurious" intrinsic = belonging to a thing by
   its very nature, genuine

 covetousness = Strong's # 4124 "avarice, fraudulency,
   extortion" avarice = greedy desire for money;
   fraud = cheat, deceit, dishonest; extortion = obtain
   money by force, fraud, or illegal use of authority

 wrath = Strong's # 3709 "desire (as a reaching forth or
   excitement of the mind), violent passion (ire, or
   (justifiable) abhorrence); punishment"

Mortify therefore your members
which are upon the earth; fornication,
uncleanness, inordinate affection, evil
concupiscence, and covetousness, which is
idolatry: For which things' sake the wrath of
God cometh on the children of disobedience:
In the which ye also walked sometime, when
ye lived in them.

Colossians 3: 5-7

In the picture:

The picture is of a believer throwing his stinking old clothes in the garbage and putting on his "new man" clothes. This came to him from the Bible, which renews his knowledge of the image of Jesus. "Image" is shown as a mirror with the cross reflected in it.

Word Definitions

3: 8-10   put off = a word used for taking off clothes

anger = Strong's # 3709 "desire (as a reaching forth or excitement of the mind) violent passion (ire, or (justifiable) abhorrence); punishment"
deep smoldering, resentful bitterness

wrath = Strong's # 2372 "passion (as if breathing hard): fierceness, indignation"   sudden outburst

malice = Strong's # 2549 "badness, depravity or malignity or trouble"
moral evil (especially here, harm caused by evil speech)

blasphemy = Strong's # 988 "vilification (especially against God)" slander

filthy language = Strong's # 148 "vile conversation"
obscene, derogatory speech intended to hurt

lie = Strong's # 5574 "to utter an untruth or attempt to deceive by falsehood"

renewed = Strong's # 341 "to renovate"   new quality

knowledge = Strong's # 1922 "recognition, full discernment"
deep, thorough knowledge

The source of knowledge is the Bible.
The goal of knowledge is to conform us to the image of Jesus.

But now ye also put off all these; anger, wrath, malice, blasphemy, filthy communication out of your mouth. Lie not one to another, seeing that ye have put off the old man with his deeds; And have put on the new man, which is renewed in knowledge after the image of him that created him:

Colossians 3: 8-10

In the picture:

This represents the matching quiz from a class. The picture shows eight people from the different groups mentioned in the verse. Even though they are all different shapes and sizes, their "new clothes" are the same. They may have started out differently, but now Christ is all and in all. All are really in the same Image. The correct matching letter will be "i" in all eight labels.

Word Definitions

3: 11   Greek = Strong's # 1672 "a Hellen (Grecian), a Greek speaking person, especially a non-Jew"   an elite

Jew = Strong's # 2453 "Judean (as a country), belonging to Jehudah"

Barbarian = Strong's # 915 "foreigners, non-Greek" inarticulate speech, warlike

Scythian = Strong's # 4658 "a savage" hated and feared invaders, the worst of the Barbarians

bond = Strong's # 1401 "slave (voluntary or involuntary; in qualified sense subjection or subserviency)"

free = Strong's # 1658 "unrestrained (to go to pleasure), (as a citizen) not a slave (whether freeborn or manumitted), or exempt (from obligation or liability)"

Christ breaks down the cultural, racial, religious, and social barriers that mankind constructs.

Renewed in Knowledge:
Image Quiz
name: _____

① __ ② __ ③ __ ④ __ ⑤ __ ⑥ __ ⑦ __ ⑧ __

Fill in the blank with the appropriate label:

A. Greek   E. Barbarian
B. Jew   F. Scythian
C. circumcised   G. slave   I. Christ in all!
D. uncircumcised H. free

Where there is neither Greek nor Jew,
circumcision nor uncircumcision, Barbarian,
Scythian, bond nor free: but Christ is all, and
in all.

Colossians 3: 11

71

In the picture:

The believer is the one "picked" by God. He receives a package addressed to him and sent from Christ, who has made us holy and beloved. Enclosed are the believer's new clothes, labeled with the qualities God wants us to put on. Love is above all these things, and it is what pulls it all together. (Trying to put on these qualities without love is legalism.)

Word Definitions

3: 12-14   Put on = "to put on clothes or envelope in"

  therefore = because of what has just been said

  elect = Strong's # 1588 "select, favorite"

      chosen by God (Eph 1:4)

  beloved = Strong's # 25 "to love (in a social or moral sense)"

  mercies = Strong's # 3628 "pity"

  kindness = Strong's # 5544 "usefulness, moral excellence (in character or demeanor)"

  humbleness of mind = Strong's # 5012 "humiliation of mind, modesty"

  meekness = Strong's # 4236 "gentleness, humility"

      the willingness to suffer injury rather than inflict it

  long-suffering = Strong's # 3115 "fortitude"   patience

  forbearing = Strong's # 430 "to hold oneself up against, put up with" to endure and not retaliate

  forgiving, forgave = Strong's # 5483 "to grant as a favor, gratuitously, in kindness, pardon or rescue" gracious

  quarrel = Strong's # 3437 "blame, fault"

  charity = Strong's # 26 "affection or benevolence"

  perfection = Strong's # 5047 "completeness"

Put on therefore, as the elect of God, holy
and beloved, bowels of mercies, kindness,
humbleness of mind, meekness, longsuffering;
Forbearing one another, and forgiving one another,
if any man have a quarrel against any: even as
Christ forgave you, so also do ye. And above all
these things put on charity, which is the bond of
perfectness.

Colossians 3: 12-14

In the picture:

The man has peace and a crown (God) in his heart. He is a believer because he loves Jesus (the cross). Because of this, he is able to have the peace of God. The long arm of God is picking him and moving him to the one cross that is filled with those who are the saved in Christ and make up one body.

He is very thankful.

Word Definitions

3: 15   peace = Strong's # 1515 "(to join); prosperity"
both an agreement or treaty, and an attitude of rest and security

Romans 5:1-2; God is not at war with believers

rule = Strong's # 1018 "to arbitrate, to govern"
like an umpire, to guide in decisions

body = Strong's # 4983 "(a sound whole)"

thankful = Strong's # 2170 "well favored, grateful"

And let the peace of God rule in your hearts, to the which also ye are called in one body; and be ye thankful.

Colossians 3: 15

In the picture:

Here we have a Bible dwelling inside a rich treasure chest labeled "wisdom" inside the man! This makes him wise and able to teach truth and warn people. His heart is full of grace. We see a page of his notes for teaching, and we see the musical notes that come from his mouth. First there is wisdom, then the emotion is shown in singing to the Lord from his heart. His song is offered to God as praise and worship for His pleasure.

The teaching of truth should lead to the emotion of singing to the Lord.

Word Definitions

3: 16   word = Strong's # 3056 "something said, topic, reasoning or motive, a computation, (Christ)"   Scripture

dwell = Strong's # 1774 "to inhabit"

richly = Strong's # 4146 "copiously"
   extravagantly, abundantly

wisdom = Strong's # 4678 "wisdom (higher or lower, worldly or spiritual)"

teaching = Strong's # 1321 "to teach, impart truth"

admonishing = Strong's # 3560 "to put in mind, to caution or reprove gently"
   to warn people of the consequences of their behavior

psalms = Strong's # 5568 "a set piece of music, a sacred ode (accompanied with voice, harp or other instrument)"

hymns = Strong's # 5215 "to celebrate"   praise God

spiritual songs = Strong's # 4152 "non-carnal, ethereal"
   a testimony
   Compare:
      Col 3:18 - 4:1 and Eph 5:19 - 6:9
   the Word dwells richly = filled with the Holy Spirit
   These are interchangeable concepts and results.

Let the word of Christ dwell in you richly in all wisdom; teaching and admonishing one another in psalms and hymns and spiritual songs, singing with grace in your hearts to the Lord.

Colossians 3: 16

In the picture:

      The man is a believer who is thanking God the Father (the crown). His praise goes through the cross (Jesus). He holds a hammer to represent his work or job. He also has a list that names areas in his life. He wants to do everything just as Jesus would want him to act.

Word Definitions

3: 17   deed = Strong's # 2041 "(to work) toil (as an effort or occupation, an act)"

    name = Strong's # 3686 "a 'name' (authority, character)"

    to act consistently with who He is (I Cor 10:31)

And whatsoever ye do in word or deed, do all in the name of the Lord Jesus, giving thanks to God and the Father by him.

Colossians 3: 17

In the picture:

A loving husband and a submissive wife are fitting in the Lord (the cross).

Word Definitions

3: 18-19   wives = Strong's# 1135 "a woman; specifically a wife"

submit = Strong's # 5293 "to subordinate, to obey"
willingly, not by compulsion, does not imply inferiority, not absolute

own = Strong's # 2398 "pertaining to self, one's own; by implication, private or separate"

husbands = Strong's # 435 "a man (properly as an individual male)"

fit = Strong's # 433 "to attain to, be proper"
an obligation, duty, how God designed the family

love = Strong's # 25 "to love (in a social or moral sense)"
continuous action, a willing love, not passion or emotion, but of choice;   covenant love = self-sacrifice; deep affection for a sister in the Lord, a weaker vessel to be cared for, a fellow heir of grace

bitter = Strong's # 4087 "to be bitter"
to act with harshness or temper, resentment; do not irritate your wife, but provide loving leadership

Wives, submit yourselves unto your own husbands, as it is fit in the Lord.

Husbands, love your wives, and be not bitter against them.

Colossians 3: 18-19

In the picture:

Here we have one family where all the members are smiling, and the children are eager to help. The children have ears that they use to listen to their parents (obey). These parents love their children and would never ask them to do anything that is against God's Word. The crown above stands for God, and the smile shows He is pleased.

The smaller picture is of a father who is reading from a LONG list of rules which he expects the children to follow perfectly. There is an X through this picture because the Lord doesn't want us to be this type of parent. Some rules are good, but the excess of rules, over-protection, nagging, or neglect of the needs of the child are not good. These things discourage and exasperate people, even children.

Word Definitions

3: 20-21   children = Strong's # 5043 "a child (as produced)" any child still living at home and under the parent's guidance

obey = Strong's # 5219 "to hear under (as a subordinate) to listen attentively; by implication to heed or conform to a command or authority"   a continuous obedience

pleasing = Strong's # 700 "(through the idea of exciting emotion); to be agreeable (or by implication to seek to be so)"

fathers = also parents

provoke = Strong's # 2042 "to stimulate (especially to anger)" exasperate, stop nagging your children

discouraged = Strong's # 120 "to be spiritless, disheartened" without courage

Obedient in "all things" that are in line with God's Word.

Children, obey your parents in all things: for this is well-pleasing unto the Lord.

Fathers, provoke not your children to anger, lest they be discouraged.

Colossians 3: 20-21

In the picture:

The scene is the demonstration of how two workers react when their master tells them to do something.

1) One worker's heart is full of "Me." He only works if the boss is watching. He says things that he thinks the boss wants to hear- even if he really doesn't believe it (his fingers are crossed behind his back). He is selfish and sneaky.

2) The other worker has ears to hear his earthly boss and then he obeys right away. He loves God, and God's Word says to be honest and true (sincerity of heart) and do what your earthly boss says --unless it contradicts His Word. (His Father in heaven sees all things all the time.)

Word Definitions

3: 22   Servants = Strong's # 1401 "to enslave"

masters = Strong's # 2962 "supreme in authority, controller"

eyeservice = Strong's # 3787 "sight-labor, that needs watching (remissness)"

menpleasers = Strong's # 441 "man-courting, fawning"

singleness = Strong's # 572 "singleness (without dissimulation or self-seeking), or generosity (copious bestowal)" sincerity

fearing = Strong's # 5399 "to frighten, to be alarmed; to be in awe of, revere"

Servants, obey in all things your masters
according to the flesh; not with eyeservice, as
menpleasers; but in singleness of heart, fearing God:

Colossians 3: 22

In the picture:

   The believer gives his hands and his heart to work for the Lord. There are two smaller figures who are looking away (no faces). The man doesn't care if they know all the work that he has done because he serves the Lord. He will receive a reward from the Lord that is his inheritance (in a treasure chest because it is so precious -Eph 1:18). This inheritance is guaranteed (Eph 1:14); eternal (Heb 9: 15); incorruptible, undefiled, doesn't fade, and is reserved for you (I Peter 1:4).

   There is another man whose heart is only filled with "Me." He has done wrong by not loving God. He is also repaid for his actions and finds only the fire of judgment, no matter who he is.

Word Definitions

3: 23-25   reward = Strong's # 469 "requital" return for any office, good or bad; in a good sense, compensation; recompense; in a bad sense, retaliation or punishment

inheritance = Strong's # 2817 "heirship, a patrimony or possession"

serve = Strong's # 1398 "to be a slave to (lit or fig, voluntary or involuntary)"

wrong = Strong's # 91 "to be unjust, do wrong (morally, socially, or physically)"

receive = Strong's # 2865 "to tend, take care of; provide for, to carry off (as if from harm; generally obtain)"

respect of persons = Strong's # 4382 "favoritism"

And whatsoever ye do, do it heartily, as to the
Lord, and not unto men; Knowing that of the
Lord ye shall receive the reward of the
inheritance: for ye serve the Lord Christ. But
he that doeth wrong shall receive for the
wrong which he hath done: and there is no
respect of persons.

Colossians 3: 23-25

87

Colossians

Chapter Four

Masters, give unto your servants that which is just and equal; knowing that ye also have a Master in heaven.

(2) Continue in prayer, and watch in the same with thanksgiving; (3) Withal praying also for us, that God would open unto us a door of utterance, to speak the mystery of Christ, for which I am also in bonds: (4) That I may make it manifest, as I ought to speak.

(5) Walk in wisdom toward them that are without, redeeming the time. (6) Let your speech be always with grace, seasoned with salt, that ye may know how ye ought to answer every man.

(7) All my state shall Tychicus declare unto you, who is a beloved brother, and a faithful minister and fellow servant in the Lord: (8) Whom I have sent unto you for the same purpose, that he might know your estate, and comfort your hearts; (9) With Onesimus, a faithful and beloved brother, who is one of you. They shall make known onto you all things which are done here.

(10) Aristarchus my fellow prisoner saluteth you, and Marcus, sister's son to Barnabas, (touching whom ye received commandments: if he come unto you, receive him;) (11) And Jesus, which is called Justus, who are of the circumcision. These only are my fellow workers unto the kingdom of God, which have been a comfort unto me.

(12) Epaphras, who is one of you, a servant of Christ, saluteth you, always laboring fervently for you in prayers, that ye may stand perfect and complete in all the will of God. (13) For I bear him record, that he hath a great zeal for you, and them that are in Laodicea, and them in Hierapolis.

(14) Luke, the beloved physician, and Demas, greet you.
(15) Salute the brethren which are in Laodicea, and Nymphas, and the church which is in his house.

(16) And when this epistle is read among you, cause that it be read also in the church of the Laodiceans; and that ye likewise read the epistle from Laodicea.

(17) And say to Archippus, Take heed to the ministry which thou hast received in the Lord, that thou fulfil it.
(18) The salutation by the hand of me Paul. Remember my bonds. Grace be with you. Amen.

In the picture:

       The believing, earthly boss deals with his servants with a Just and Equal treatment. He remembers that God, who is his Boss, treats him with a Just and Equal treatment. He has a responsibility to deal rightly with others... just as he would want to be treated.

Word Definitions

4: 1   Master = Strong's # 2962 "supreme in authority, controller"

servant = Strong's # 1401 "to enslave"

just = Strong's # 1342 "equitable (in character or act) by implication innocent, holy"

equal = Strong's # 2471 "likeness (in condition or proportion)" fair

Masters, give unto your servants that
which is just and equal; knowing that ye also have
a Master in heaven.

Colossians 4: 1

In the picture:

This picture shows the Colossians praying earnestly and alertly (with their eyes open).

1) One is praying with thankfulness to God.

2) Another is asking God (the crown) to open a door (give Paul an opportunity) to preach God's Word. Remember to pray with courageous persistence! Paul doesn't ask God to "open unto us a door" so that he can escape, but that even in prison he would have more opportunity to preach Christ. (Paul is able to write Colossians, Ephesians, Philippians, and Philemon while in prison.)

3) The next figure is asking God to help Paul speak the mystery (the question mark) of Christ (the cross). This mystery is the gospel for which Paul has been put in prison.

4) The last figure is asking God to help Paul preach clearly and speak as he ought to speak (*boldly* from Eph 6:19 and *in love* from Eph 4:15). The picture shows the curtain with the question mark being pulled open to reveal the cross. God is making the hidden purpose of the cross apparent. This purpose is the gospel of Christ, that is, Jesus' innocent death on the cross for payment of the believer's sins.

Word Definitions

4: 2-4   continue = Strong's # 4342 "to be earnest toward, to persevere, be constantly diligent, or (in a place) to attend assiduously all the exercises, or (to a person) to adhere closely to (as a servitor)"

courageously persistent to hold fast and not let go

watch = Strong's # 1127 "to keep awake"

alert to specific needs

mystery = Strong's # 3466 "a secret (through the idea of silence imposed by initiation into religious rites)"

something hidden in the Old Testament that is revealed in the New Testament

manifest = Strong's # 5319 "to render apparent (lit or fig)"

make clear or plain

ought to speak = to speak as God wants him to speak

Colosse church

Continue in prayer, and watch in the same
with thanksgiving; Withal praying also for us,
that God would open unto us a door of utterance,
to speak the mystery of Christ, for which I am
also in bonds: That I may make it manifest, as I
ought to speak.

Colossians 4: 2-4

In the picture:

This figure is walking in a channel of wisdom. The references along the side mention ways of gaining wisdom. The clock has been rescued (another meaning for redeemed) because it has value for him. There are no hands on the clock because he doesn't know how much time is left to him. His speech is "grace" with a salt shaker adding the seasoning. This makes his words more palatable and preserving. The figure is walking toward the group of people who are outside the walkway of wisdom. They are unbelievers because they have no heart full of love for Jesus. They are watching the Christian and are wanting answers for the questions they have about his unusual life.

Word Definitions

4: 5-6   redeeming = Strong's # 1805 "to buy up, ransom, to rescue from loss (improve opportunity)"

grace = Strong's # 5485 "graciousness (as gratifying) of manner or act (abstract or concrete, literally, figuratively, or spiritual; especially the divine influence upon the heart, and its reflection in the life, including gratitude)"
joy, pleasure, delight; sweetness, charm, loveliness, spiritual, wholesome, fitting, purposeful, truthful

seasoned = Strong's # 741 "to prepare, spice (with stimulating condiments)"

salt = Strong's # 217 "salt; fig, prudence"
stinging, preserving, flavoring, purifying

Walk in wisdom toward them that are
without, redeeming the time. Let your speech be
always with grace, seasoned with salt, that ye may
know how ye ought to answer every man.

Colossians 4: 5-6

In the picture:

Paul is sending Tychicus and Onesimus on a long trip to deliver Paul's letters (Colossians, Philemon, and probably Ephesians). These letters are in the mail bags. Paul wants to let these churches know how he is doing and to find out how they are faring. He wants to comfort their hearts because they are probably worried about Paul (the hearts in the church show concern).

Word Definitions

4: 7-9   Tychicus = Acts 20:4, Eph 6:20, 2 Tim 4:12, Titus 3:12
a fellow servant
faithful = Strong's # 4103 "trustful"
fellow servant = Strong's # 4889 "a co-slave, servitor or ministrant of the same master (human or divine)"
comfort = Strong's # 3870 "to call near, invite, invoke (by imploration, exhortation, or consolation)"
Onesimus = Philemon 10;   a runaway slave, now saved (Philemon = one of the leaders in the Colosse church and Onesimus' master)

directions from Rome to Colosse:
cross Italy on foot
sail across the Adriatic Sea
cross Greece on foot
sail the Aegean Sea to Asia Minor
walk 100 miles inland to Colosse

TYCHICUS
· faithful servant

ONESIMUS
· runaway slave
from Colosse

All my state shall Tychicus declare unto you, who is a beloved brother, and a faithful minister and fellow servant in the Lord: Whom I have sent unto you for the same purpose, that he might know your estate, and comfort your hearts; With Onesimus, a faithful and beloved brother, who is one of you. They shall make known onto you all things which are done here.

Colossians 4: 7-9

In the picture:

Aristarchus is with Paul in prison, but he isn't really chained. He is there to aid Paul. He is waving a greeting to the Colosse church.

Marcus is the writer of the gospel of Mark and the relative of Barnabas. Paul reminds the Colossians to welcome Mark because he has become quite a helper to Paul, even though he started out undependable.

Justus (Jesus was his other name) is another Jewish helper who has been a comfort to Paul.

They are Jewish Christians working for the kingdom (shown as the castle) of God (shown as the crown).

Word Definitions

4: 10-11   Aristarchus = a Jewish believer from Thessalonica Acts 19:29, 20:4, 27:2, and Philemon 24

fellow prisoner = Strong's # 4869 "a co-captive" one caught with a spear; probably not an actual prisoner, but choosing to stay with Paul

Marcus = John Mark, relative of Barnabas and the author of the gospel of Mark; Philemon 24; I Peter 5:13; He deserted Paul and Barnabas on their 1st missionary journey, but grew to be one of Paul's best helpers. Paul instructs the Colossians to welcome Mark and not hold his past against him.

Barnabas = many references from Acts 4:36 through 15:39; I Cor 9:6; Gal 2:1, 9, 13

commandments = Strong's # 1785 "injunction, an authoritative prescription"

Justus = a Jewish acquaintance of Paul

comfort = Strong's # 3931 "an address alongside, consolation" encouragement

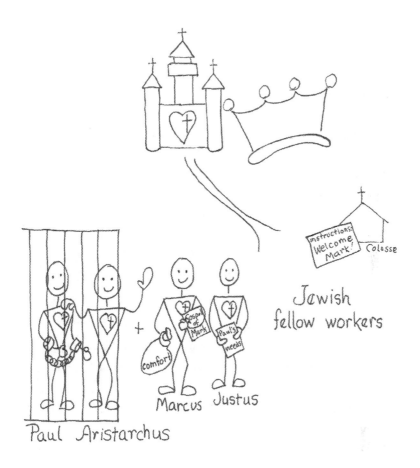

Aristarchus my fellow prisoner saluteth you, and Marcus, sister's son to Barnabas, (touching whom ye received commandments: if he come unto you, receive him;) And Jesus, which is called Justus, who are of the circumcision. These only are my fellow workers unto the kingdom of God, which have been a comfort unto me.

Colossians 4: 10-11

In the picture:

Epaphras is on his knees praying because he is always praying, especially for the three churches from his home area. He is probably the pastor of the Colossian church. He is shown waving his greeting to them. His thoughts and prayers are that God would help the churches stand completely and entirely in all the will of God. He agonizes for them in his prayers as shown in the drops of sweat that dot his forehead.

Paul testifies of the zeal and ardor (burning heat, enthusiasm) that Epaphras has for his people.

Word Definitions

4: 12-13   Epaphras = Colossians 1:7, Philemon 23; from Colosse, probably the founder of the Colossian church and possibly its current pastor

saluteth = Strong's # 782 "to enfold in the arms, to salute, to welcome"

fervently laboring = Strong's # 75 "to struggle, lit (to compete for a prize) or generally (to endeavor to accomplish something)"   agonize

record = Strong's # 4137 "to be a witness, testify"

zeal = Strong's # 2205 "properly, heat, (fig) zeal (in a favorable sense, ardor; in an unfavorable one, jealousy, as of a husband (fig of God) or an enemy, malice" great energy or enthusiasm in pursuit of a cause

Laodicea = the chief city of Phrygia

Hierapolis = a city in Phrygia

Epaphras, who is one of you, a servant of Christ, saluteth you, always laboring fervently for you in prayers, that ye may stand perfect and complete in all the will of God. For I bear him record, that he hath a great zeal for you, and them that are in Laodicea, and them in Hierapolis.

Colossians 4: 12-13

In the picture:

The picture shows the last two of Paul's fellow workers. Dr. Luke is beloved. He waves his greeting. However, Demas is a sad case. Here he is a helper, but he will abandon Paul and the ministry later. He is a double-minded man. His heart was not filled with love for Christ. He also greets the far away church of Laodicea and the church that meets at Nymphas's home.

Word Definitions

4: 14-15   Luke = 2 Tim 4:11; a Gentile believer who was Paul's doctor and friend. He penned the Gospel of Luke and Acts

physician = doctor of medicine

Demas = 2 Tim 4:10; Philemon 24; Later he deserts Paul and the ministry

Nymphas = a Christian from the Laodicean area; some manuscripts make it a woman's name

church = Strong's # 1577 "a calling out, a popular meeting, especially a religious congregation (Jewish synagogue, or Christian community of members on earth or saints in heaven or both)"

Luke, the beloved physician, and Demas,
greet you. Salute the brethren which are in
Laodicea, and Nymphas, and the church which
is in his house.

Colossians 4: 14-15

103

In the picture:

The two churches are exchanging their letters after having read them. The Laodicean letter is a bit of a mystery. It is probably the letter of Ephesians.

Word Definitions

4: 16   epistle = Strong's # 1992 "a written message"

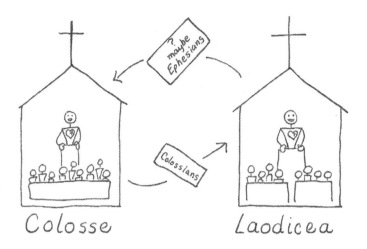

And when this epistle is read among you, cause that it be read also in the church of the Laodiceans; and that ye likewise read the epistle from Laodicea.

Colossians 4: 16

In the picture:

Paul himself is writing his closing remarks in his letter from prison. He is still in chains. He is thinking of the message he wants Archippus to hear. He wants to encourage him to work for the Lord. He ends his letter with an "Amen" which means "so be it."

Word Definitions

4: 17-18　　　Archippus = Philemon 2; perhaps Philemon's son

heed = Strong's # 991 "to look at (lit or fig)"

ministry = Strong's # 1248 "attendance (as a servant);fig (eleemosynary) aid, (official) service (especially of the Christian teacher, or technically of the diaconate)"
　　　eleemosynary= of, relating to, or dependent on charity; charitable (from "alms" and "compassion")

fulfil = abundantly supplied

salutation = Strong's # 783 "a greeting (in person or by letter)"

remember = Strong's # 3421 "to exercise memory, recollect; by implication, to punish; also to rehearse"

bonds = Strong's # 1199 "a band, ligament (of the body) or shackle (of a prisoner), fig an impediment of disability"

Amen = Strong's # 281 "firm, trustworthy, surely, so be it"

And say to Archippus, Take heed to the ministry which thou hast received in the Lord, that thou fulfil it.
The salutation by the hand of me Paul.
Remember my bonds. Grace be with you. Amen.
Colossians 4: 17-18